# THE SIERRA CLUB
# ENDANGERED SPECIES POSTCARD COLLECTION

## INTRODUCTION BY GEORGE SCHALLER

Sierra Club Books

The Sierra Club, founded in 1892 by John Muir, has devoted itself to the study and protection of the earth's scenic and ecological resources—mountains, wetlands, woodlands, wild shores and rivers, deserts and plains. The publishing program of the Sierra Club offers books to the public as a nonprofit educational service in the hope that they may enlarge the public's understanding of the Club's basic concerns. The point of view expressed in each book, however, does not necessarily represent that of the Club. The Sierra Club has some sixty chapters coast to coast, in Canada, Hawaii, and Alaska. For information about how you may participate in its programs to preserve wilderness and the quality of life, please address inquiries to Sierra Club, 730 Polk Street, San Francisco, CA 94109.

A note to the correspondent: these slightly oversized postcards require the same postage as a first-class letter.

**Library of Congress Cataloging-in-Publication Data**

The Sierra Club endangered species postcard collection.

1. Rare animals—Pictorial works.   2. Endangered species—Pictorial works.   I. Sierra Club.
QL82.S54   1988     591′.042     88–42552
ISBN 0–87156–790–3

Front cover: Jaguar, Manu Nat'l Park, Peru, by Warren Martin Hern.
Editor: David Spinner
Production: Susan Ristow
Cover design: Bonnie Smetts
Book design: Bonnie Smetts
Printed by South Sea International Press Ltd., Hong Kong

10 9 8 7 6 5 4 3 2 1

# Introduction

Mountain gorilla, snow leopard, giant panda, whooping crane — their noble portraits adorn calendars and crown books, an endless parade of endangered species. Never has more attention been paid them, yet ironically never has their future been more uncertain. Icons of our culture, such animals elicit more passive appreciation than active concern for their living beauty and outrage for their plight. Already they seem to represent memorials, as if their drama has ended, as if already they have joined the dodo, great auk, and passenger pigeon. So many images of the dying almost lessen the intensity with which extinction is viewed; capacity for concern is finite.

Protesting such destruction is now a moral imperative; forgetting is a luxury we cannot afford. Yet too often we mourn only the decline of such charismatic creatures as the blue whale or black rhinoceros, and ignore the myriad of tiny and modest organisms, whether insects or worms, who unobserved are also turning from splendor to dust. We are in an extinction spasm rivaling that of the Cretaceous period 65 million years ago, when two-thirds of all species, including the last dinosaurs, vanished. But unlike that silent cataclysm, the current one is man-made, the result of a large human population squandering its resources, sacrificing the eternal for the expedient.

The unobtrusive species have the most important functions in an ecosystem, the plants that produce nutrients and the soil bacteria and fungi that decompose them. And even the most insignificant species represents an essential genetic storehouse, offering us potential food, drugs, and other services. By contrast, the loss of a spectacular animal from the wild, such as the California condor, may actually be more a moral and aesthetic tragedy than an ecological one.

Still, the extinction of the lion seems more of a loss than would that of the leech. Majestic species have a spiritual resonance, they have become totems, often symbols of particular eco-systems. By protecting the elephant and quetzal we also save thousands of other species in the same habitat.

In the final analysis, the real battle is less to save the black-footed ferret than to shape new attitudes, to create a new design in the strategy of human survival. Photographs and biographies of endangered species not only remind us of their existence, but also of today's most urgent issue: to conserve the diversity of life. "What is life?" asked Crowfoot, a Blackfoot Indian, in 1890. "It is the flash of a firefly in the night. It is the breath of a buffalo in the winter time. It is the little shadow which runs across the grass and loses itself in the Sunset."

George Schaller
*Wildlife Conservation International*

*Editor's note:* As used in this collection, the term "endangered" refers to species that have been designated as endangered, threatened, or vulnerable, in all or part of their distribution, by the U.S. Fish and Wildlife Service and/or the International Union for the Conservation of Nature (IUCN). The locations indicated in the captions refer to the site where the animal was photographed and not necessarily those geographic locations in which the animals are most threatened.

David Spinner
*Sierra Club Books*

African elephants *(Loxodonta africana),* Wankie
National Park, Zimbabwe.

Gray wolf *(Canis lupus),* Jasper National Park,
Alberta, Canada.

Tigers *(Panthera tigris),* native to temperate and
tropical Asia. National Zoo, Washington, D.C.

Bald eagle *(Haliaetus leucocephalus)*, Chilkat River,
Alaska.

Orangutan *(Pongo pygmaeus)*, Sumatra.

Snow leopard *(Panthera uncia),* native to central Asia.
Bronx Zoo, New York.

American crocodile *(Crocodylus acutus)*, Belize.

Humpback whales *(Megaptera novaeangliae)*, Maui,
Hawaii.

Japanese macaques *(Macaca fuscata)*, Shiga Highlands,
Japan.

Jaguar *(Panthera onça),* Manu National Park, Peru.

Brown pelican *(Pelecanus occidentalis)*, Florida.

Brown bear *(Ursus arctos)*, Afognak Island, Alaska.

West Indian manatees *(Trichechus manatus),* Crystal
River, Florida.

Cheetah *(Acinonyx jubatus),* with cubs, Amboseli
National Park, Kenya.

Chimpanzee *(Pan troglodytes)*, Kagera National Park,
Rwanda.

Western giant eland *(Taurotragus d. derbianus)*,
Lichtenburg Nature Reserve, South Africa.

Giant panda *(Ailuropoda melanoleuca),* Szechuan, China.

Pygmy hippopotamus *(Cheorpsis liberiensis)*, West Africa.

Florida panther *(Felis concolor coryi)*, south Florida.

Andean condor *(Vultur gryphus)*, Argentina.

Gorilla *(Gorilla gorilla)*, Zaire.

Black rhinoceros *(Diceros bicornis)*, Masai Mara
National Reserve, Kenya.